MW01222819

Nature's MINIBEASTS

Honeybees

Clint Twist

GARETH**STEVENS**
PUBLISHING
A Member of the WRC Media Family of Companies

Please visit our web site at: www.garethstevens.com
For a free color catalog describing Gareth Stevens Publishing's list
of high-quality books and multimedia programs,
call 1-800-542-2595 (USA) or 1-800-387-3178 (Canada).
Gareth Stevens Publishing's fax: (414) 332-3567.

Library of Congress Cataloging-in-Publication Data

Twist, Clint.
      Honeybees / Clint Twist. — North American ed.
          p. cm. — (Nature's minibeasts)
      Includes index.
      ISBN 0-8368-6376-3 (lib. bdg.)
      1. Honeybee—Juvenile literature I. Title.
   QL568.A6T85   2006
   595.79'9—dc22   2005044713

This North American edition first published in 2006 by
Gareth Stevens Publishing
A Member of the WRC Media Family of Companies
330 West Olive Street, Suite 100
Milwaukee, WI 53212 USA

This edition copyright © 2006 by Gareth Stevens, Inc. Original edition copyright © 2006
by ticktock Entertainment Ltd. First published in Great Britain in 2006 by ticktock Media Ltd.,
Unit 2, Orchard Business Centre, North Farm Road, Tunbridge Wells, Kent TN2 3XF.

Gareth Stevens series editor: Gini Holland
Gareth Stevens graphic designer: Dave Kowalski
Gareth Stevens art direction: Tammy West

Photo credits (t=top, b=bottom, l=left, r=right, c=center): FLPA Images: 8-9 all, 11 all.
Science Photo Library: 15r, 17t, 18-19 all, 20b, 21t.

Every effort has been made to trace the copyright holders for the photos in this book. The publisher apologizes
in advance for any unintentional omissions and would be pleased to insert appropriate acknowledgements in
any subsequent edition of this publication.

Printed in the United States of America

1 2 3 4 5 6 7 8 9 10 09 08 07 06

Words that appear in the glossary are printed in
boldface type the first time they occur in text.

 # Contents

What Are Honeybees?

Honeybees are medium-sized, winged **insects**. They look furry, and they make a tell-tale buzzing sound when they fly. Honeybees can deliver a painful sting, and they make **honey**!

How do honeybees live?

Honeybees belong to a group of insects known as social insects. They live in a very large family group called a **colony**. Most of the honeybees in a colony are **workers** that collect **nectar** and **pollen** from flowers.

Honeybees live in nests called hives.

Insects belong to a group of **minibeasts** known as **arthropods**. Adults have jointed legs but do not have an inner **skeleton** made of bones. Instead, they have tough outer skin, called an **exoskeleton**, that supports and protects their bodies. All adult insects have six legs. Most also have at least one pair of wings. Honeybees have two pairs.

Where do honeybees live?

Honeybees live wherever there are plenty of flowers for at least some months of the year. Honeybees do not like cold conditions, but they do not like hot, dry weather, either.

What do honeybees eat?

Honeybees eat nectar and pollen from flowers and resin, or tree sap, from trees. They are excellent flyers and can check a flower for pollen while **hovering** in midair. If they do not see any pollen, they just fly on to the next flower.

The small back wings of honeybees are hidden under their front wings.

A Honeybee Up Close

Most worker honeybees are about ½ inch (16 millimeters) long and have six legs and two pairs of flying wings. A layer of fine hairs makes this minibeast look fuzzy. It is divided into three parts — head, **thorax**, and **abdomen**.

thorax

head

abdomen

The abdomen is the largest part of the honeybee's body. It contains the **digestive system** and other important **organs**.

A special organ, called the honey-stomach, lies inside the upper abdomen. Nectar is stored here instead of passing through the bee's digestive system.

The bee's head holds its **antennae**, eyes, mouth, and brain. The honeybee's legs and wings are attached to the middle part of its body, the thorax.

SIX LEGS

Bees and other insects are sometimes called hexapods because they have six legs. (*Hex* means six in Latin.) All insects are hexapods, but not all hexapods are insects. A honeybee is an example of a hexapod. A springtail is a hexapod, but it is not an insect.

Like all other hexapods, honeybees have six legs.

Hive Home

A honeybee colony is a huge family with thousands of closely related members. The colony builds a nest called a hive. The hive is a very busy and highly organized place.

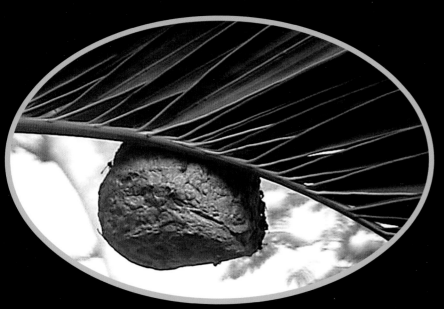

A honeybee hive hangs on a leaf.

Honeybees often build hives in trees. Bees may build a hive on a branch if they cannot find a hollow. If trees are in short supply, the bees will build hives under roofs, on or below the ground, in old termite mounds, or in caves. Each hive has three types of bees — workers, **drones**, and a **queen**.

① Most honeybees (about 50,000 per colony) are **infertile** females called workers.

② Each colony has a single **fertile** female bee that rarely leaves the hive. She is the queen bee, and she lays all the eggs for the colony. Workers feed the queen bee royal jelly.

③ Drones are male bees. They are bigger than worker bees but smaller than the queen bee. They do not bring food to the hive. Their only purpose is to mate with the queen, if they can catch her.

TREASURE HOUSE

A hive not only provides a home, it is also the colony's treasure house. The hive holds the queen bee, the growing larvae, and the colony's precious store of food. In order to protect these treasures from being spoiled by bad weather or **intruders**, workers bees often construct a wall of solid mud around the entire hive.

This bee hive is protected by a casing of mud.

9

Queen Bees

Queen bees are the largest honeybees. They are about .7 inches (18 millimeters) long. A queen mates only once in her life. Drones **fertilize** the queen during a mating flight. Then the queen lays eggs for the hive.

The queen lays thousands of eggs a day for the rest of her life. Fed and cared for by worker bees, she never leaves the hive again except to start a new hive, or to escape from danger.

A queen bee can control how her eggs develop. Most eggs develop into worker bees. The colony always needs new workers because most workers live for only a few months.

A queen bee is the largest bee in the hive.

A queen bee inspects a cell in her hive.

The queen occasionally lays eggs that hatch into drones. A queen honeybee lays "queen eggs" only when the colony needs a new queen.

A queen bee pupa rests in its cell.

KILLER QUEENS

When it is time for a new queen, the old queen lays several queen eggs at the same time. Queen eggs are fed royal jelly and are given careful treatment. The first of the eggs to hatch and form a **pupa** usually becomes the next queen. The first thing a new queen does is sting to death all the other queen pupae before they come out of their **cells**.

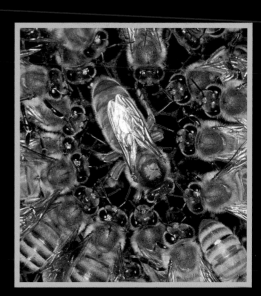

Worker honeybees surround a queen honeybee. There is room for only one queen in a hive.

Cells of Life

The inside of a hive is a great example of insects' building skills. Worker bees have made each cell out of **beeswax.** Each cell has six sides that are especially well-shaped to fit together.

In the hive, the queen lays her eggs, dropping each egg into an individual cell. After the queen lays the eggs, the workers cap and seal each cell with wax.

Worker bees cap the egg-filled cells with wax.

Inside a cell, the egg hatches into a **larva,** which looks a little like a caterpillar. The larva is the young form of a bee. All the **larvae** are fed and cared for by workers. Workers uncap the cells, feed the larvae, and then reseal the cells.

This close-up photograph shows a bee pupa.

When a larva reaches its full size, it forms an outer casing around itself. At this stage in its life, a bee is known as a pupa. Inside the casing, the pupa changes into the body shape of an adult. Then, the fully formed young bee comes out of its cell.

A young bee has just come out of its cell.

INSECT DEVELOPMENT

Insects develop from eggs in two different ways. Many insect eggs, including those of bees, hatch into wormlike larvae. The larvae then go through a stage called **pupation**, during which they change into adults. The eggs of many other insects hatch into **nymphs** that already have adult body shapes.

Honeybee larvae look like small worms or caterpillars.

Repairs and Guard Duty

After a young worker bee comes out of its cell, it spends about two weeks inside the hive. Its first duties include taking care of the cells.

Young workers keep the cells in good repair and make new ones from wax. Worker bees produce small amounts of wax in special **glands** on the sides of their abdomens.

A young worker bee repairs cells in a hive. The cells must be kept in good condition so they will be ready when the queen needs to lay eggs inside them.

The workers use their legs to scrape this wax into small balls that can be carried around the hive. They chew the wax to make it sticky, shape it in their mouths, and press it into place.

A young worker bee's head looks scary!

Then the young bees move on to guard the hive. Their job is to keep out intruders, which range from insects and other minibeasts to birds and mammals. While on guard duty, guard bees flutter their wings at the entrance, creating a light wind that helps cool the inside of the hive.

These guard bees are ready to sting any intruder that attempts to enter the hive.

STING AND DIE

When a worker honeybee stings an intruder, the worker dies. The bee's stinger has **barbs** that catch on the victim's flesh and hold the stinger firmly in place while the bee injects poison into the victim. When the worker pulls out the stinger, the stinger tears away from the bee's abdomen. The worker bee dies soon afterward.

The used stinger of a worker honeybee shows it will die soon.

Finding Flowers

Honeybees look for plants with lots of flowers because flowers make pollen and nectar. When bees collect pollen and nectar, they help many plants make seeds.

Flowers do not make pollen to feed bees. Flowers produce pollen so that one flower can fertilize another to produce seeds that will grow into new plants. As honeybees collect pollen for food, they help the plants by dropping pollen when they fly from flower to flower.

Grains of pollen from a flower stick to the hairs on a bee's body. Some of this pollen falls off onto other flowers as the bee travels. This action is called pollination.

This close-up view shows a pollen grain.

Bees have excellent eyesight, but they can only see in ultraviolet (UV) light. UV light is a part of the light spectrum, like X-rays, that humans cannot see. Flower petals often have patterns designed to attract honeybees. These patterns are invisible to humans.

Bees use ultraviolet light to see flowers.

SWEET TASTE

A flower's pretty patterns might be enough to attract bees, but many plants also produce small amounts of sweet, sugary nectar. Bees and many other insects find this high-energy food especially appealing. Nectar is a honeybee's favorite food.

The sweet nectar in flowers attracts honeybees.

Doing the Waggle Dance

Each morning that plants are in flower, specially selected scout bees are sent out to find the best sources of pollen and nectar. Any worker can be a scout bee, but usually, the older, more experienced bees are chosen.

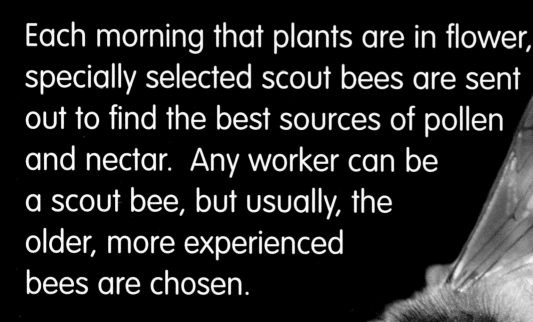

Scout bees fly up to about 2 miles (3 kilometers) in all directions from the hive to look for newly opened flowers. When each scout returns to the hive (*left*), it reports what it has found by doing the waggle dance.

Returning scouts do this figure eight dance at the hive's entrance. The central path of the dance shows other bees which direction they should go to find the pollen and nectar.

The speed of the dance steps, the number of times the scouts do the steps, and the speed of their fluttering wings during the dance all share information, such as the distance, the amount, and the quality of the pollen and nectar.

HONEYBEE NAVIGATION

Honeybees navigate, or find their way around, by using the Sun. Not only do bees use the Sun's direction, but they also use the height of the Sun in the sky and the strength of sunlight as it changes during the day. This information helps honeybees know exactly where they are, even when their hive is out of sight.

Honeybees use the Sun to find their way to the best flowers and back to their hive.

19

Busy Bees

For most of their short lives, worker bees collect pollen and nectar every day. Most of what they collect goes to meet the colony's daily need for food. The many young bees, larvae, and the queen must all be fed. Extra food is stored.

Workers collect pollen with their mouths and front legs and carry it back to the hive in special pollen baskets on their back legs. Any nectar they collect is carried inside each worker's special honey stomach.

This close-up photo shows a worker bee's mouthparts.

The honeybee's pollen basket is full of pollen.

MAKING HONEY

Inside a hive's individual wax cells, the bees' nectar and pollen mixture slowly dries out into a sticky substance called honey. The collection of close-fitting honey cells is called a **comb**. The special six-sided, or hexagonal, shape of the cells works well to fit many cells tightly together in a small space.

Any food that will not be eaten right away is stored in empty egg cells that have been cleaned. Workers squirt any spare nectar from their honey stomachs into a cell, and add any extra pollen they may be carrying. Then they seal the cell.

Honeybees collect resin (*right*) to protect their honeycombs.

Honeycomb is made up of closely packed, six-sided wax cells with thin walls.

Besides pollen and nectar, honeybees also collect water, which all animals need, and the sticky resin, or tree sap, which they use for sealing the ends of their honey cells.

Honeybees and Humans

Many animals enjoy the taste of honey, and some even enjoy the taste of bees! Human beings like the taste of honey so much, they found ways to raise and keep honeybees more than five thousand years ago.

People all over the world keep honeybee hives and harvest the honey. They build hives for a bee colony out of mud, braided straw, or wood. Because the beekeepers feed their bees, they are able to remove all the stored honey, and the bees will still survive.

Two beekeepers inspect colonies of Russian honeybees.

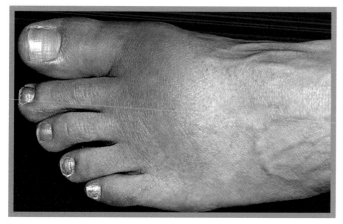

The venom injected when a bee stings causes redness, pain, swelling, and itching.

Beekeepers are careful to protect themselves from being stung. They often wear veils for protection. Each bee sting contains a tiny amount of mild poison. Only a few people, who are allergic to bees, are badly affected by a single sting, but lots of stings can inject a dangerous amount of poison.

A beekeeper's hat and veil help provide protection against stings.

CANDLELIGHT

Beekeeping provides people with more than just honey. For thousands of years, fine candles have been made from beeswax, which burns brightly and has a nice smell. Today, most candles are made from wax that comes from crude oil, but beeswax is still used for the finest and most expensive candles.

The wicks on these beeswax candles must be cut apart before they can be lit.

Different Bees

Scientists have counted about forty thousand species of bees. Most bees do not live in large colonies the way honeybees do. Some live in smaller colonies. Some live all by themselves. All bees eat nectar and pollen, but no bees except honeybees build up such big stores of honey.

Bumblebees

Most bumblebees are much bigger, hairier, and noisier than honeybees. Unlike honeybees, bumblebees are able to sting more than once. Bumblebees have warning colors, such as black and yellow or black and red. They live in far smaller colonies than honeybees, with a queen and some twenty to two hundred family members. Only the queen, however, survives the winter. She survives by **hibernating** in a burrow.

Carpenter Bees

A carpenter bee is about the size of a bumblebee. The female carpenter bee uses the hard point of her stinger to chip out many narrow holes in pieces of dead wood. At the bottom of each hole, she lays a few eggs. Even a single carpenter bee can do a lot of damage to wood furniture.

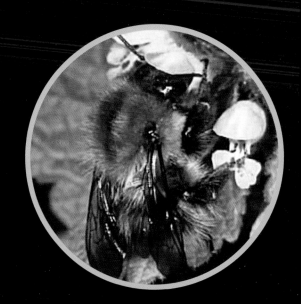

Cuckoo Bees

Cuckoo bees are solitary bees, which means they live by themselves. The are **parasites** on other bees. Cuckoo bees do not build nests. Instead, a female cuckoo bee finds the nest of another species of solitary bee and invades it. The female cuckoo bee stings to death all the eggs and larvae before cleaning out the cells. Then she lays her own eggs in these stolen cells.

Leaf-cutter Bees

Leaf-cutter bees also live by themselves. They have powerful **jaws,** which they use for cutting leaves and tunneling into soil. After digging a tunnel, the female cuts round pieces from the leaves of nearby plants. She rolls each piece into a tube and puts it inside the tunnel. Then she lays an egg in each "leaf cell." She seals the cells up with pollen and nectar that will feed the larvae after the eggs hatch.

Bee Mimics

Bees can sometimes be hard to identify because many other insects look like bees. Some insects that look like bees can even get inside a hive without being stung by guard bees at the hive's entrance. Minibeasts that copy, or mimic, the appearance of bees are known as bee mimics.

Drone Flies

The drone fly belongs to a group of flying insects known as hover flies, many of which are bee or wasp mimics. Drone flies look just like harmless honeybee drones, but they are not harmless. They sneak into honeybee hives to feed on stored pollen.

Greater Bee Flies

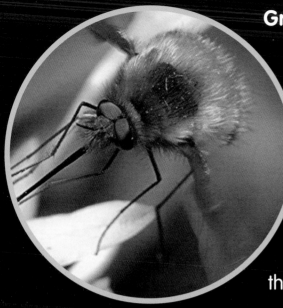

The greater bee fly looks just like some bee species except that is has a long mouthpart called a proboscis. It uses its proboscis like a drinking straw to feed on nectar. Females scatter their eggs while flying around. When the eggs hatch on the ground, the fly larvae look for the nests of solitary bees and eat the bee larvae.

Velvet Ants

This minibeast has the hairy appearance of a bee, and is called an "ant," but it is really a species of wasp. Velvet ants are even more dangerous parasites than cuckoo bees. The females lay their eggs inside the bodies of bee larvae and pupae. When the velvet ant larvae hatch, they eat the developing bees.

Bumble Flies

Like other hover flies, the bumble fly does not sting. It hopes that its predators think it is a bumblebee, which has a strong, sharp stinger. Like bumbelbees, bumble flies feed on nectar and pollen.

Life Cycle

Three types of honeybees live inside each colony. Queens produce eggs. Drones, or males, mate with the queen to make baby bees. Workers, which are females that cannot have babies, take care of the hive and bring food to the hive. The kind of food that workers feed each larva decides the type of adult the larva will become. Larvae fed with royal jelly become drones if they are males and queens if they are females. Larva that are fed only pollen and nectar become workers.

2 Egg hatches into a larva, which is fed by worker bees.

1 Queen lays an egg in a cell.

3 Larva grows and changes into a pupa.

4 Pupa develops into an adult honeybee.

worker

queen

drone

Fabulous Facts

Fact 1: About twenty thousand species of bees exist, but only about four are considered true honeybees.

Fact 2: Honeybees have been raised by people since the age of the pyramids, about five thousand years ago.

Fact 3: Honeybees started in tropical Africa and spread from southern Africa to northern Europe and east into India and China.

Fact 4: The first fossil bees date back about forty million years and are almost identical to modern bees.

Fact 5: Each honeybee colony can have tens of thousands of bees inside. Some colonies contain as many as eighty thousand honeybees.

Fact 6: A queen may live two to five years, but drones usually die before winter. Most workers live only a few months.

Fact 7: A queen makes only one mating flight during her lifetime. She mates with up to twenty drones on that single flight. Drones that mate with her die in the act.

Fact 8: Worker bees eat pollen to produce bee milk, which is sometimes called royal jelly. They feed royal jelly to the queen all her life and to drone and queen larvae for three days after they hatch from their eggs. Worker bee larvae are fed a mixture of pollen and nectar called bee bread.

Fact 9: A queen is fed a high protein food produced by young workers. This food helps her lay up to two thousand eggs a day, or about twice her body weight.

Fact 10: Scientist Karl von Frisch studied the behavior of honeybees. Von Frisch noticed that honey bees do the waggle dance to "talk" to each other. He was awarded the Nobel Prize for physiology and medicine in 1973.

Fact 11: Drone bees do not have stingers. The queen bee can sting many times, but she rarely needs her stinger, except to kill rival queens.

Fact 12: If a colony gets too big for one queen, she will lay several queen eggs. When a new queen comes out of her larva cell, the old queen will fly away from the hive with some of her workers and start a new colony.

Glossary

abdomen — the largest part of an insect's three-part body, which holds most of its important organs

antennae — a pair of special sense organs found at the front of the head on most insects

arthropods — minibeasts that have jointed legs, including insects and spiders

barbs — sharp hooks on a bee's stinger

beeswax — a sticky, solid substance that honeybees produce in their bodies and use to build storage cells for their food and eggs

cells — hollow, six-sided units made by honeybees, in which they lay their eggs, raise their young, and store honey and other food

colony — a large group of insects, or other living things, that live together

comb — a collection of beeswax cells built side by side within a hive

digestive system — the organs in an animal's body that are used to process food

drone — a male bee

exoskeleton — a hard outer covering that supports and protects the bodies of some minibeasts

fertile — able to produce babies

fertilize — to put pollen from one plant onto another to make seeds or to combine a male seed with a female egg to make new life

glands — parts of an animal's body that produce particular substances the animal needs

hibernating — living through the winter by going into a state of rest or inactivity

honey — sweet, syrupy substance made by bees from pollen and nectar

hovering — flying in one place

infertile — not able to produce any babies

insects — minibeasts with six jointed legs, three-part bodies, and usually also one or two pairs of wings

intruders — any living things that enter a place where they do not belong or are not invited

jaws — hinged mouth structures that help most animals bite and chew

larva/larvae — the form of certain young insects after hatching from an egg. More than one larva are called larvae.

minibeasts — any of a large number of small land animals that do not have skeletons inside their bodies

nectar — a sugary liquid produced by flowering plants and used by honeybees to make honey

nymphs — the young of insects that do not produce larvae, which look like small adults after hatching from eggs

organs — parts of an animal's body that perform particular tasks, such as the stomach, which digests food

parasites — living things that live, depend, or feed on the bodies of other living things without giving anything useful in return

pollen — the tiny grains produced by flowers, to fertilize other flowers

pupa/pupae — the form of an insect that is in the process of changing from a larva into an adult. More than one pupa are called pupae.

pupation — the process by which many insect larvae change their body shapes to adult forms

queen — the largest honeybee in a colony and the only bee in the colony that can lay eggs

skeleton — an internal structure of bones that supports the body of an animal

thorax — the middle part of an insect's body, to which the legs are attached

workers — female honeybees that cannot produce young and are the main type of bees in a hive

Index